THE ROYAL CANADIAN MOUNTED POLICE

illustrated by
MARC TETRO

Scholastic Canada Ltd.
Toronto New York London Auckland Sydney
Mexico City New Delhi Hong Kong Buenos Aires

Thanks to Malcolm J. H. Wake, director of the
Museum of The Royal Canadian Mounted Police,
for his help during my visit to Regina;
to Victoria Wonnacott, my assistant, for her meticulous research;
and finally, to Dale Horeczy, my partner,
who assisted in every aspect of the publication of this book.

Scholastic Canada Ltd.
604 King Street West, Toronto, Ontario M5V 1E1, Canada

Scholastic Inc.
557 Broadway, New York, NY 10012, USA

Scholastic Australia Pty Limited
PO Box 579, Gosford, NSW 2250, Australia

Scholastic New Zealand Limited
Private Bag 94407, Botany, Manukau 2163, New Zealand

Scholastic Children's Books
Euston House, 24 Eversholt Street, London NW1 1DB, UK

Library and Archives Canada Cataloguing in Publication
Tétro, Marc, 1960-
The Royal Canadian Mounted Police / written and illustrated by Marc Tetro.
Translation of: La Gendarmerie royale du Canada.
ISBN 978-1-4431-0779-2
1. Royal Canadian Mounted Police--History--Juvenile literature. I. Title.
FC3216.2.T4713 2011   j363.20971   C2011-902377-6

Marc Tetro and Martin Loranger co-authored the text of the French edition of this book
which was used in part in preparing this English edition.

Graphic design: Christopher Cant

6 5 4 3 2 1   Printed in Singapore 46   11 12 13 14 15

To all the grandparents
who've ever wanted to tell the story
of the Royal Canadian Mounted Police
to their grandchildren.

THE ROYAL CANADIAN MOUNTED POLICE

More than
a hundred years ago,
on the vast
Canadian prairie,
lived the country's
first people.

They lived in teepees,
houses they could
quickly pack up
when they wanted to follow
the herds of bison.

At that time,
John A. Macdonald,
Canada's first
prime minister,
dreamed of uniting
the country's
West with the East.
He decided to build a railway.

To help him
accomplish this,
and to look after the people
who would work on it,
a group of capable men
was put together.
They were called the Mounted Police.

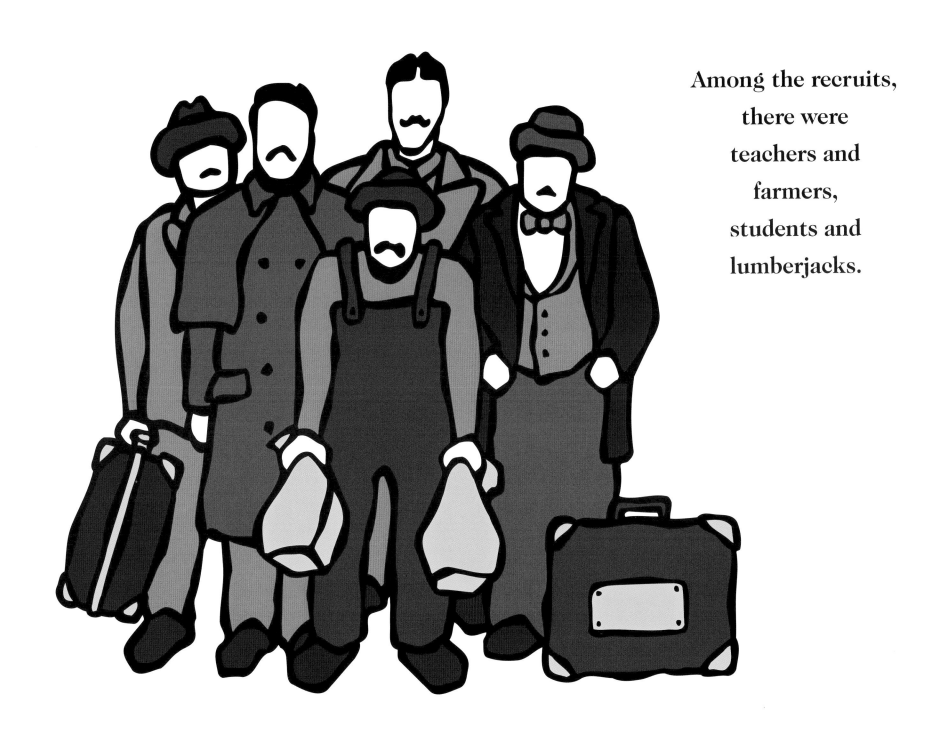

Among the recruits, there were teachers and farmers, students and lumberjacks.

The proud new Mounties were eager for adventure as they set out from Manitoba for their long journey West. The land was beautiful, and it seemed to go on forever. But it was also cruel. The sun burned down, the sky was filled with black-flies . . .

. . . and the animals were exhausted.

Finally, after two long months, the cavalcade reached the land of the Blackfoot.

The Mounties immediately
went to work building
their first outpost
in the West:
Fort Macleod.

With time, some of the Blackfoot elders
learned to trust these men in red tunics,
and an agreement was reached.
The train would now be allowed
to cross their land.

Later, Louis Riel, the leader of the Métis,
a people of French and Indian blood,
fought the division of his ancestors' land.
The Métis wanted their own country, but their dream was not to come true.

The workers began building the railway.

Soon, the first whistle of the Canadian Pacific train blew in the West. The train brought people from eastern Canada, as well as Ukrainians, Poles and Germans from Europe.

There were houses to build,
fields to plough and a new way of life to learn.
The Mounties were there to help
the new families settle in.

The Mounties'
musical ride
entertained the
people in the
new communities.

Gold in the Klondike!
Thousands of men
rushed to the Yukon
hoping to strike it rich.

Dawson City went mad.
Men used
bad language,
played cards
and spent the night
dancing with the ladies.

But, of course,
the law
had to be
respected.

The Mounties
reached the Far North.
There, they met the Inuit.
These people
snuggled up in igloos,
houses that were
made of blocks of ice.
It was the Inuit who helped
the Mounties explore
the Canadian Arctic.

King Edward VII
recognised
the important work
the Canadian Mounties
were doing,
and he gave them
a royal title.

They become known as the Royal North-West Mounted Police. Later, their name was changed to the Royal Canadian Mounted Police.

Today, the Mounties
don't travel the country on horseback
as they did in the time of
John A. Macdonald.
But their work is just as important:
they're dedicated to
protecting Canadians by watching
over the country's borders,
from the Atlantic Provinces
to the Yukon.